in a world of wishes

dane thomas

i

All people have a time to begin, and a time to end; but the most important part is the time in between each beginning and each ending, for that is the time they take our hand and lead us, they take our mind and teach us, and they take our heart and love us. This book is dedicated to my Grandfather who dedicated his life to teaching and inspiring people to follow their hearts and pursue their dreams.

Contents

1. in my eyes

I feel as though every person under the sun has a purpose, and maybe you haven't found yours yet, but I need you to understand that your existence is important; and if no one has ever told you that before, I want you to know your life is important to me.

And here you are, unsure of yourself, because they constantly look beyond all the things you have to offer the world, and only choose to see your imperfections.

The world would be quite different if we spent a little more time listening and comprehending, and a little less time judging the things we don't understand.

She was chaos mixed with
beauty, and sunshine mixed
with the fiercest storm.

Your purpose is so much more than being an average person living a normal life.

Settling will never be the answer; not for life, love, or your own happiness, because settling simple means you have given up on what you believe you deserve.

The problem is you're real, and they don't know how to handle someone with depth and soul like you.

I know how easy it is to close the world out, but there are so many people waiting for you to tear down your walls and open the door.

I would rather be the person who was respected for showing my flaws to the world, than be the coward who hides amongst the crowd because they are ashamed of who they are.

I hope you never feel like your life needs to move as slowly or as quickly as everyone else in the world. We all experience things differently; set your own pace.

She is beautiful in a way the world doesn't understand, for the world only understands what the eyes can see; but the beauty she has is the rarest of all, for it's the type you feel with every part of your soul.

Not everyone was designed to
see the magic in your madness.

Do you know what I love most about people? Our differences, it's what makes us so interesting. I love the way your nose crinkles when you laugh, or the way your tattoos tell the stories of who you are. And do you know what I hate most about people? How we think we are never good enough. We see people in magazines and wish, just for a moment we could be them, and that's so messed up. We tend to forget that life isn't about money, looks, or fame, it's about embracing the life we've been given, and living it to the absolute fullest.

Don't let appearances fool you,
some of the ugliest humans I
have ever known came
wrapped in the most beautiful
skin.

Find someone who will let you
run wild, but also knows how
to lead you back home.

One day you'll wake up and all your time will be gone, so stop waiting to live, because the time for that is right now.

Sometimes it's overwhelming
to be human; to feel the world
spinning around you while you
stand in silence in the moment.

Don't ever let someone make
you feel inadequate just
because they don't understand
you.

I know you've been searching for that person who shakes up your life and rattles your soul, but maybe you need to look a bit closer, because that person is you.

There is a difference between being alive and living, one is just existing, the other is allowing yourself to feel.

The ocean doesn't sit calmly and wait for the world to tell it which direction to move; neither should you.

And though our appearances are different, beneath the skin there is a heart that beats in us all, and even if that's the only similarity we have, it's enough to remind us that we are all human, perfectly flawed in our own unique way.

My entire life I was told
heaven and hell were just a
place, but as I've grown older
I've found that it isn't just a
place, for they both can be
found in people.

The hands on the clock move
as the hours pass slowly, yet
the days fade away and quickly
turn into years, and in time you
will change, as the world will
too, for nothing is meant to
stay the same.

The world is in despair because we constantly let hatred overpower love.

2. heartstrings

I believe life breaks us all with tragedy, pain, and heartbreak. Life will tear you apart many different times, but don't you dare let your heart grow cold; there are so many people who have love to offer you, so don't give up on them.

You deserve someone who is real and genuine with the way they love, someone who is truthful in the things they say and someone who always chooses you, no matter what.

She was my drug and
I was her whiskey,
she was drunk on love,
and I was addicted.

If I had to choose my favorite part of every day, I would always choose the time I get to spend with you.

Maybe forever is
just a miracle away,
maybe your forever
starts today.

They asked me what I thought love was, and I said, it's fighting to keep someone when everything in the world tries to tear you apart. It's holding someone at 2 a.m. when they're sick. It's accepting someone for their light, but also understanding their darkness. It's sacrificing what you want, to give them what they need. It's embracing the happiness, but being strong through the pain. Love isn't always beautiful, sometimes it's chaos, but love is holding on through the good and bad, and assuring them you'll never let go.

If they truly love you, you'll never have to question it, for it will show through their actions, not just their words.

Be the type of person you don't have to convince yourself to love.

Time takes its toll on the body,
so make sure you fall in love
with their mind.

I know you're afraid, but you have got to understand that not everyone gets the opportunity to love, so if you get the chance, take it.

If they are willing to fight everything in the world to keep you, when they tell you they love you, believe them.

When this moment ends,
I hope it ends with your hand
in mine, with our hearts
entangled for the rest of time.

If you want to find love
that's truer than true,
you've got to find someone
who loves you for you.

When life got complicated, you
reminded me that love could
still be simple; that two people
could exist in a world full of
chaos and still make it to the
end of time.

Be genuine in the way you love these people that surround you, for even though it seems as if the time is passing by slowly, our lives are passing by quickly.

You won't fall in love with the person who always sees your smile; you'll fall in love with the person who finds you in the pouring down rain, picks you up, and holds you until the storm passes.

Some people change the way you see, others change the way you feel, and if you get lucky, you'll find someone who does both.

Maybe these days will turn into months, and these nights will turn into years, and this love that we share will be endless.

She loved in a way that was so fearless, she left pieces of her heart in everything she touched.

You caught me off
guard on a summer day,
when my heart was cold
and the skies were gray,
your eyes had a spark
I couldn't resist,
you made me light up
with just one kiss.

I'll make you believe
every single day,
that love is real,
and it's here to stay.

And maybe that's all we need;
a little love that lasts a lifetime.

In this time, and in this place, I want you to be unforgivably yourself; full of flaws, beauty, chaos, and imperfection, for these are the things that make you real, and the things that are real in this world are the things I love most.

When the world ignites and the sky falls, when the clocks stop and the stars grow dim, I'll be there with you, and I swear I'll love you until the end.

There I was stripped of all the things the world had given me, left with nothing else to give, and you found me, and gave me a piece of your heart, so I could begin to live again.

I will love your flaws in the same way I love your beauty. I will love your mind as much as I love your heart. I will love you through the happiness, and hold you through the sadness. I will love you, every single part of you, and I can promise you that.

You'll know it's real when you see the scars but choose to help them heal, when you see the tears but choose to wipe them away, and when you see the ugliest parts of someone but choose to stay; because that's what love is, it's holding on even when things get tough, and assuring them you won't let go.

You will meet people who
come and go and it won't
phase you, but others will find
you, and they will change you;
they'll change your
perspective, they'll change
your life, and the most
important thing is, they'll
change your heart.

Tell them you love them over
and over again. Tell them too
much and never too little, for
the time we have is short, but
the love we have is endless.

I hope somewhere out there
you can find someone who you
can create a love with that even
the hands of time can't break.

Even forever wouldn't be long enough, as long as I'm with you.

3. happiness

Here is my heart and my
happiness, please be careful
with how you use them.

I used to think the key to life
was success, but as I've grown
older I realized I had it all
wrong; the key to life is
happiness.

And that's all it takes; two souls that bond together, and the chaos of their worlds fade away.

Don't ever let the cruel things in this world take away your happiness.

You are constantly searching for happiness, yet the journey to happiness starts with you, and how you choose to love yourself.

Take the risk, take the chance, make mistakes. Go to the ocean, hang out with friends, tour the city, climb the mountain, because that's what life is about; it's about taking time to live in these moments that you will never get back.

When their voice calms your demons, and their eyes show you hope for the future, you'll know you've found what you have been searching for all along.

Everyone has a little spark of madness in them; I hope you ignite yours and let it burn wild.

If you aren't happy, I hope you have the courage, right here, right now, to leave whatever you find to be unsettling.

Be the type of person who ignites happiness in someone's soul.

I remember the way things were, the way I thought I was full of life and love; and then there was you, and you changed everything, and I felt what it was like to be genuinely happy, and I never looked at life in the same way again.

It took me a long time to realize my happiness needs to come first, and maybe that's selfish, but so is someone expecting you to spend your entire life unhappy to please themselves.

Someday you will be first; the first thought on someone's mind when they wake up in the morning, the first person they search for in a crowd, the first real love, the first person they want when the tears are streaming down their cheeks, the first person they call when joy overwhelms them. You'll be the first person for everything, and then you'll understand why you never settled for being second.

Never give up on your search
for happiness; your life
depends on it.

Maybe we're just
a heartbeat away,
from loving the
life we live today.

I hope you get to a part in your life that is so good you never want it to end.

She wore one thing that turned heads in any light of day, she wore happiness in the most pure and genuine way.

If there is one
thing that will
always hold true,
it's the belief that
you were meant for me,
and I was meant for you.

Let the sparks of magic in your soul light up your world like the stars in the night sky.

Did it ever occur to you that you should be a little less concerned about things, and a little more concerned with your happiness.

We will travel to mountains
and the oceans so blue,
we will drink and be merry,
just me and just you.

I hope you find your happiness;
not just the kind of happiness
you see in a smile, the kind you
feel with every part of your
being.

There is someone in the world whose happiness resides in you; don't forget that.

4. pain

She would let her heart
turn cold as ice,
before she'd let a fool
break it twice.

You will fall victim to the
tragedies of life, but some of
the most valuable lessons
you'll learn are the ones you'll
learn in the midst of pain.

There is a time to stand still and embrace the moment, and there is a time to ignite the fire in your soul and live.

They will hate you for
everything you are, for that is
what jealousy does to people, it
makes them hate the things
they will never become.

Stop swimming in the shallows
and let your love find its depth
in a place where there is no
end.

These lies you keep telling
yourself about how you don't
deserve to be loved are what
keep your heart caged.

One day you wake up and you're an adult and life is difficult, and it's challenging, and no one is there to save you; and you have got to know how to save yourself.

You've lived out the modern
tale of Romeo and Juliet many
different times; you just never
realized lies were the poison,
and words were the dagger,
that fatally ended two star
struck lovers.

I've been misused and
misplaced, I am tattered, torn,
and rough around the edges,
but you never saw any of those
things; you only saw all the life
that was still left in these
broken pieces of me.

The battle is challenging, and it won't be fair, but you have to understand that life is always worth fighting for.

I've picked myself up off the floor more times than I could bear to tell; and every time I whisper to my heart, "try one more time, I swear we'll get it right next time."

Sometimes it's in the way we
fall apart that truly helps us
find ourselves; for when we are
broken, we can arrange our
pieces in any way we choose.

Don't tell me you love me if you are willing to break my heart to satisfy your own.

If there is one thing I will never understand, it's how someone can walk out of your life and pretend the bond you shared for so long never existed.

Sometimes I remember a moment in time when everything was perfect, and so many different times I wished just for a minute, I could return to that place, and that time, and live it once more.

And maybe that's how
it suddenly ends,
two people break
instead of bend,
our pieces begin to
shatter and fall,
and we lose our hearts
in the midst of it all.

You have to understand that
people have their time and
place in your life, and
sometimes life requires that
time to run out.

It isn't worth losing yourself to fight for a heart that will never belong to you.

I don't expect you to
understand how life has broken
me, I just need you to see that
these pieces of who I am are
still so full of life.

Those who fall to the depths of pain are the one who arise as the most extraordinarily beautiful beings of all.

This addiction went
straight to her veins,
she got drunk on love
and it healed the pain.

There will be some that never truly see the way the stars shine, they lose sight of the way the sun beams glow in the darkest of hours; and that's why they look at you, and fail to see your beauty.

We build walls and close doors
because we simply fear what
the unknown future holds. We
hide our hearts, and bury our
feelings deep beneath the
surface so we don't have to risk
the pain that can often come
with love; and it's such a shame
we've come to this, for if we
open up our minds and hearts
to chance, there are countless
opportunities that lie behind
the door.

If I must fall and shatter into a million pieces before I can become the best version of myself, then let me fall.

When my entire world went up in flames, and everyone left me to burn, you stayed, because you would rather set yourself on fire than exist in a world without me; and God only knows how much I needed someone like you.

5. hope

You won't find your purpose as quickly as everyone else, for you must search for who you are, before you find what you are to become.

We are all here, in the middle of our story, embracing this life, and wondering where the world will take us next.

I hope you always look at me like it was the first time you saw me, when the butterflies in your stomach went wild, and the sparks in your soul ignited.

I know how hard it is to walk
away, but in the end,
sometimes letting go is the
only way to save yourself.

Life was never meant to be completely understood, for if we understood everything, we would never have the opportunity to learn.

I understand how the world can burn. I've seen the stars grow dim, and I've seen how the summer rain can wash away memories of the past. I've seen the way the trees fall apart in the September breeze, and I've seen the way the snowflakes shimmer as they melt in the light of the December sun; but despite it all, I still believe a single star can light the darkness, that rain can cleanse even the most painful things, that the trees in September show how endings can be beautiful, and that even the coldest hearts can be melted by the warmth of love.

You will never quite understand where you belong until you follow your heart to where it truly needs to be; and that's when you will understand that home isn't necessarily a place, it's the feeling of being exactly where you were meant to be.

You are living proof that a broken heart can be fixed, that intuition can change the world, and that imperfection can be beautiful.

Maybe it's the madness in me that still makes me believe two hearts can connect, and ignite magic that only the hands of time can break.

If you ever meet an angel with tarnished wings, you'll know they moved heaven and hell to save you.

Someday you will meet someone who never asks you to change, they will see every one of your flaws and still think you're perfect for everything you are; this is the person that will breathe life back into your tired soul, and remind you that miracles do still exist.

When your soul finds its match
your feelings will align with
theirs, for when they feel pain
your heart will break with
theirs, but when their heart is
filled with love, it will be the
most extraordinary feeling, for
your heart will be overflowing
with love too.

Her beauty wasn't reflected
in a mirror full of lights,
it didn't come from clothing
with price tags a fright,
her beauty was found
deep from within,
for that is where all
true beauty begins.

And sometimes the memory fades, but the heart holds treasures the mind can't begin to contain.

If you want to be great, you have to understand that falling a few times is what makes you strong.

My favorite people are the
ones who still have soul,
the type that still have hope
when the world grows cold.

Perfection only exists in those who see their flaws as beautiful.

Stars will never fail to light the night sky, no matter how many people tell them they aren't bright enough.

The strongest people are the ones who have rebuilt themselves from the ashes of the things that tried to destroy them.

There is a certain type of magic
that finds its way into our lives
at the perfect moment; and that
type of magic is often found in
people who enter our lives at
the most unexpected times.

You will find your own freedom when you stop letting them chain you down with their opinions.

I'm not here to tell you life will be easy, for I know the difficulties you face. I'm here to tell you it's pain and tears, and bruises and scars, but that's why you were built to be strong.

We often forget that the moon and stars hang in the sky above our head, the grass whispers in the wind below our feet; and we are here in the middle of it all, just small beings in such an extraordinary place.

6. journey

And like the sun, we all must rise and fall, for our destiny is found between the two.

Would the world still love you if they saw you for who you really are? No deception, no masks, no lies; just facts. See that's the thing about people, we hide our imperfections behind so many different things. We show the world our smile, yet we choose to hide our scars. It's like telling half of our story, and burning the pages we don't think they would understand.

They try to destroy what they don't understand, and that's why they want to destroy who you are. They can't stand the thought of someone bringing the purity of authenticity into a world ruled by corruption.

This is your journey, it isn't meant to be understood by everyone, for it is yours, and yours alone.

Five years from now you'll
regret the trip you didn't take,
the career you failed to pursue,
and the person you didn't find
the time to visit.

This is your life, and I'd be so disappointed in you if you lived it the way someone else chose for you.

Every moment in time leads you to the exact place you are meant to be, and maybe you won't understand the reason now, but you will someday.

They'll tell you to fit in, to follow the crowd, but I hope you never do. I hope you always choose to run at your own pace, on the path your heart chooses to lead you.

You will be a whirlwind of chaos to some, but to others, you will be the calm to their storm.

She will never be the type of woman who lets someone calm the wild within her; so if you want to love her, you've got to run wild with her.

Your voice is the most powerful thing you possess; don't be afraid to use it.

One day there will be someone
who you'd cross oceans to see,
you'd fight anything in the
world to save, and you'd give
up everything to keep.

I often found myself making decisions based on other people's opinions, and it took me a long time to realize how foolish that was.

We are all born with a spark of
magic in us, it's what gives us
the power to dream and the
hope that allows us to believe
in the things we can't always
see; the problem is, as we grow
up, some of us lose our spark.

It's pain and heartbreak, it's happiness and love, it's hopes and dreams, it's sunshine and rain; it's this beautiful chaos we call life.

I will never be like them,
nor will I ever try to be,
I am perfectly misplaced,
in a world that doesn't see.

In falling you learn to stand on your own two feet, you learn that your own strength is one of the most valuable things you possess, and you learn that no matter what, the way you love yourself is one of the greatest loves of all.

Maybe who you are lies in
something a little more real,
not just in the way you look,
but in the way you make
people feel.

One day you will understand
that these memories you hold
so close, are pieces of every
person you've ever had the
chance to love.

Good or bad, happy or sad, I'll always be here. I won't distance myself when times get tough, or run at the first sign of things not being perfect. I will embrace every ounce of this life with you, no matter where life leads us. I will always be here, and I can promise you that.

And maybe they don't deserve
it, but forgive them anyway,
because you deserve to let go
of the things that weigh on
your mind and hold you back
from your own happiness.

I know you're a mess because
life has taken its toll on your
heart, but I hope somewhere
out there you can find the love
you need to carry on.

It's in our darkest hours that we see people for who they truly are, for it takes more than time to save someone who is losing their battle, it also takes love.

Stop believing the people who tell you that you're incomplete. Not everyone needs another half to be whole, some of us are strong enough to carry on alone; and there is nothing wrong with that.

Someday you and I will find
our place under the star filled
sky, and happiness will
surround us; and everything
will be perfect, just like we
always planned it would be.

7. endings

I let myself fall apart with no
way of piecing it back together,
and that's why I understand
that some things will always be
broken; but that doesn't mean
broken can't be beautiful too.

And maybe in the end we will
remember each other for more
than what we were.

We define broken as being damaged or weak, yet broken can mean so many different things. Sometimes we don't bend, we break, but that doesn't mean we give up hope and throw it all away; for broken is an opportunity to learn, to start over, and to figure out what truly matters.

I never knew that would be the last time; the last time I would hear your voice, the last chance I would get to look into your eyes, or the last time I would truly feel your presence. But I now understand that life can take two people down separate paths at any given time, and one may never find their way back home.

There will come a point in time where you must walk away from the people you once knew, and the person you once were, in order to become the person the world needs you to be.

If the world ever takes us in separate directions, you'll search for me in every crowd, in every place, and in every lover who follows.

If it doesn't challenge you, change you, empower you, or love you, let it go.

And that's the way it goes
sometimes, two hearts fall
apart just as quickly as they fell
for each other.

When the dust settles and my body becomes a part of the earth once more, know that in every second, with every breath, I lived.

And we are here in this time, and in this place, living for these moments that we will never get back.

Sometimes you need silence, for not all things need to be heard; some things require us to feel.

You'll beg and you'll plead and
your heart will feel sore, but
it's hard to find love when the
world is at war.

You have got to understand that you are trading your time for the things you do each day, and maybe that doesn't seem to matter right now, but fifty years from now it will.

The moon still cries to the stars
for the love they only share in
the darkness of the night.

Maybe in the end we will be different people in a different world, and we will love each other the way we always swore we would.

Life made me experience
tragedy to remind me how
strong I really was; but that's
the thing about life, it gives and
it takes, and in the end we are
left with the memories of what
was, and the hope for what is
to come.

And maybe this is where it ends, where two hearts that once ran wild together go their separate ways; and it's something we can't stop, nor should we ever try to, for some hearts aren't meant to run at another's pace, but are meant to run wild until they can run no more.

Leave these things,
leave this place,
leave it all,
if that's what it takes.

All these things that surround you become a part of who you are; that's why you feel as if you have lost a piece of yourself when people find themselves absent from your life.

And if you must go, take a piece of my heart with you, so you never forget the love it holds for you.

Those who have walked the path with broken promises and shattered dreams are the ones who arise with the strongest wings.

8. change

I will help you tear down your walls and we will rebuild them into an extraordinary place with open doors and open windows, for I know the beauty of the soul you keep hidden, and it is time for the rest of the world to see it.

When you fall to pieces
I will take your hand
and hold you close
until you're whole again.

Find someone who makes you forget all the people in your past who made you feel unworthy.

The people who change the world the most are generally the ones who are the most misunderstood by the people who surround them.

It's quite simple the way we exist, the way we live for each day and thrive in the moments that make us feel alive; yet life has become complicated, because love turned into text messages instead of written letters, and the thrill of a little attention overpowered commitment.

There have been times that I've had to leave everything I've ever known because my heart was in a different place, and although I couldn't explain it, I trusted myself enough to follow it.

The world will take, but it will also give, and you have the opportunity to do the same. So take a little less, and give a little more, because somewhere in the world there is someone in need of the light of hope you have to share.

Be the person who is so soul shaking, you change the way the world sees.

Sometimes the only strength you need is the strength to let go of the things that are causing destruction in your life, whether it is emotionally, physically, or both; just know you are worth every bit of happiness the world has to offer, and don't ever let anyone tell you otherwise.

The truth is, you were designed to be different on purpose, for the world needed someone who makes ripples of change, and less people who let the water lie calmly while life passes them by.

They will take pieces of you as they go, and they will leave pieces of themselves behind, and that is why we change. We change because we are stitched together with mismatched pieces of chaos and beauty from every soul we have ever loved.

I promise I will love every part of you, even the parts that are broken.

I like change because it's what I fear more than anything. It's the opportunity to start over, it's the chance to pursue my dreams, and it's the possibility that I could find everything I've been searching for.

If you build walls and close the
doors to the world, you not
only choose to shut out society,
but you slowly shut out the
people who love you as well.

The world is moving so quickly, yet I am here in this moment with you, wishing for it to never end.

Our minds change, our lives change, and our hearts change, for all of these things were never meant to stay the same.

Most believe magic is just an illusion, something you see with your eyes that plays tricks on your mind; but when you find the right person, magic becomes a reality, because you won't just see it, you'll feel it in every part of your being.

The flower that blooms in the midst of the storm is always the most beautiful, for even though its petals and leaves are ripped and torn by the chaos of life, it still continues to grow.

I hope your eyes never fail to
see the beauty in this world,
and if they do, I hope you
change the way you see.

I will always fall out of place and out of line. I wasn't made to fit a mold or blend in with a crowd. I will always be unforgivably me, and no one will ever change that.

There is nothing wrong with
the way you were made, there
is just something wrong with
the way the world misconstrues
your beauty and turns it into
something so ugly.

A change in your perspective
will change your mindset; a
change in your mindset will
change your life.

I'll find you, and I will take you
to a place where the sun is
shining and the birds are
singing, and we will lay down
in the warm summer grass and
watch the clouds go by; and we
will be happy, just you and I, as
the world passes us by.

Seek adventure and new beginnings. Travel to new places and have conversations with people who are different from you. Take the time for morning coffee and afternoons with friends; for it's through these experiences that you will begin to understand yourself, and what you truly require to feel fulfilled.

The world has a way of
bringing two souls together
that were meant to intertwine,
and maybe it's fate, or maybe
it's our destiny, but I'm grateful
you and I were given the
chance to find each other.

I want to be that place you go
when you are tired and weary
from the day, the place you feel
safe and secure; where your
secrets stay hidden and your
love lives beyond your years. I
want to be that place, the place
you call home.

Follow Dane Thomas on these social media accounts:

Instagram @ dthomasquotes
Twitter @ dthomasquotes1
Facebook @ dthomasquotes

Other books by Dane Thomas

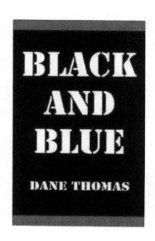
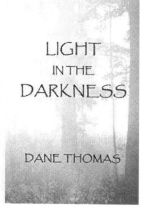

Both available on Amazon.com

Made in the USA
San Bernardino, CA
16 June 2020

73618491R00132